D1372179

#WeCanDoBetter

PART 1 | HEALING THE RACIAL DIVIDE

TONY EVANS

MOODY PUBLISHERS
CHICAGO

All Scripture quotations, unless otherwise indicated, are taken from the *New American Standard Bible*®, Copyright © 1960, 1962, 1963, 1968, 1971, 1972, 1973, 1975, 1977, 1995 by The Lockman Foundation. Used by permission. (www.Lockman.org)

Scripture quotations marked (NIV) are taken from the Holy Bible, New International Version®, NIV®. Copyright © 1973, 1978, 1984, 2011 by Biblica, Inc.™ Used by permission of Zondervan. All rights reserved worldwide. www.zondervan.com.The "NIV" and "New International Version" are trademarks registered in the United States Patent and Trademark Office by Biblica, Inc.™

Edited by Karen L. Waddles
Interior and Cover design: Erik M. Peterson

All websites and phone numbers listed herein are accurate at the time of publication but may change in the future or cease to exist. The listing of website references and resources does not imply publisher endorsement of the site's entire contents. Groups and organizations are listed for informational purposes, and listing does not imply publisher endorsement of their activities.

ISBN 978-0-8024-1181-5

We hope you enjoy this book from Moody Publishers. Our goal is to provide high-quality, thought-provoking books and products that connect truth to your real needs and challenges. For more information on other books and products written and produced from a biblical perspective, go to www.moodypublishers.com or write to:

Moody Publishers
820 North LaSalle Boulevard
Chicago, IL 60610

3 5 7 9 10 8 6 4 2

Printed in the United States of America

CONTENTS

INTRODUCTION

The racial problem is the unresolved dilemma of America. It is the asterisk on the otherwise respectable reputation of American exceptionalism. Whether manifesting itself overtly in conflicts between differing racial and cultural groups, or simply lurking below the surface as a suspicion camouflaging the true depth of the problem, it continues to be the one dominant area of our failure as a nation.

Racial problems have continued since America's inception because their root has not been addressed by the people who are most qualified to address it: followers of Jesus Christ. When we only bring people together in a limited way, without full acceptance of who they have been created to be, how can we expect much more from the world?

In spite of our successes in religion, science, education, medicine, and technology, becoming truly "one nation under God" continues to elude us.

IN SPITE OF OUR SUCCESSES IN RELIGION, SCIENCE, EDUCATION, MEDICINE, AND TECHNOLOGY, BECOMING TRULY "ONE NATION UNDER GOD" CONTINUES TO ELUDE US.

Nowhere is this more evident than in the history and contemporary reality of black/white relations in the culture at large and in the church in particular. While this tension can also be seen in many other ways, whether through swastikas painted on synagogues or Hispanics marching against the concern of racial profiling and the passage of immigration legislation, it is the black/white relationship that has set the bar of racial division the highest.

It is the black/white history that propelled the devastating tragedy of the Trayvon Martin death to the forefront of our national conversations and psyche. Whether a completely accurate comparison or not, it awakened generations of compound grief stemming back to Emmett Till, the 16th Street

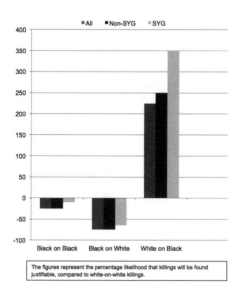

The figures represent the percentage likelihood that killings will be found justifiable, compared to white-on-white killings.

1

Baptist church bombing, and the collective groans of countless unnamed victims of injustice.

It reinforced the unwritten rule that provocation cannot be responded to without extreme penalty for one race, in particular, a rule backed up even today by the recent PBS publication of research on FBI crime data from 2000–2009 (the most current years for which data is available; see chart). These findings clearly show the likelihood of innocence or guilt swaying based on the racial identifications of both victim and aggressor.

A dialogue from the movie *42* on the life of the first African-American major league baseball player summarizes what so many have had to live with for far too long.

Jackie Robinson: "You want a player who doesn't have the guts to fight back?"

Branch Rickey: "No. I want a player who's got the guts *not* to fight back."

This expectation, while productive on many accounts, has also stoked the volcanic heat beneath the surface; when someone takes a hit so many easily identify with the lava overflows. Likewise, when voices have been silenced, explained away, or snuffed out during decades and centuries of injustice, a tsunami is unleashed, as that which engulfs us today.

A single case then becomes the recurring climax of a continuum.

Too often, though, the issue remains unresolved despite the raw honesty of emotions and communications brought to light with each high-profile issue involving race, simply

ONLY WITH A RETURN
TO BIBLICAL TRUTH
AS OUR OVERARCHING
STANDARD BY WHICH ALL
ELSE IS MEASURED WILL
AN ACCURATE VIEW OF
RACIAL UNITY BE SEEN
AND ACTUALIZED.

🐦 #WeCanDoBetter

because we have two sides who are viewing the same incident from two very different perspectives. A lot of people are talking, yet precious few are listening; so neither side seems to hear the other at all. Eventually the talking and protests simmer down and little has been changed. The cycle repeats as we all wait for another situation to once again stir the embers lying just beneath the surface.

TWO SIDES IN EVERY STORY

In the beginning, God created a man. Within the seed of that man rested all of the components, DNA, and characteristic trademarks of all people today. *In the beginning, we were one.* Scripture tells us in the book of Acts, "He made from one man every nation of mankind to live on all the face of the earth" (17:26). Thus, sharing a common origin in Adam, any form of division or oppression predicated on race is illegitimate, because we all emanate from the same source.

Racism in our society as well as in the church came about as a result of a divergence from this key biblical truth. It was not only supported by false theology, but it was also reinforced by pseudoscience, which was used to justify slavery by suggesting that people of the black race were inferior to those of the white. When theology joined hands with science, this created a double problem in the church by giving both religious and scientific support to the dehumanization and dividing process. Only with a return to biblical truth as our overarching standard by which all else is measured will an accurate view of racial unity be seen and actualized.

A major obstacle to overcome in understanding and engaging in racial unity, though, is the question of who's in charge: the Bible, science, or one's culture? This leads to a multiplicity of issues, one of which is the hindrance that is caused when authority is given to cultural diversity over biblical truth.

For example, some black Christians so mix the tenets of black culture with their faith that they frequently fail to make the necessary distinction between the two when it comes to critiquing ourselves. Many times racial hindrances are blamed for blocking forward progress either academically or vocationally. While these hindrances should be acknowledged and addressed, we must also take responsibility for ourselves, in spite of obvious hindrances, and find a way to execute at the level that we should in order to overcome them.

Conversely, whites will often leave the Bible when it is culturally convenient to do so in order to protect their traditions. This is seen most clearly in the sacred cow of interracial dating and marriage. When these issues are discussed, the argument of culture comes up as well. Questions such as: *What about the kids* and *What will the relatives think* surface much quicker than questions of what the Bible says.

On one side we have the complicated effects of traumatic and systemic grief stemming from the oppression of a people group throughout the better part of our history as a nation. The effect of this oppression is an unhealed wound that becomes easily irritated and reopened when there are acts—either actual or perceived—that resurrect or serve as a reminder of what initially caused it in the first place.

On the other side, we have a generation of people who did not participate in the evil of overt racism, and who do not control the systems that may be continuing to keep it alive today. They argue that it is unfair to pass the hostilities of these histories on to them. And they also wonder why such a huge response is made with regard to Trayvon Martin while hundreds continue to die by gunshot wounds in Chicago—sometimes more than a dozen weekly—while no collective outrage is heard.

There are questions on both sides.

In the midst of these questions, we also find those who have either been warped by whiteness or those who have become blinded by blackness to such a degree that even listening to the other side seems nearly impossible. We are left in a stalemate with regard to a strategic plan for a solution.

A BIBLICAL PERSPECTIVE

It is my contention that the fundamental cause of racial problems in America lies squarely with the church's failure to come to grips with this issue from a biblical perspective. And it is also my contention that the strategy to solve it lies within the church as well.

The truth that has been missed is that God chooses much of what He does predicated on what His church is or is not doing (Deuteronomy 4:5–8, Ephesians 3:10). In the same way that God's purpose, presence, and power in the Old Testament was to flow from His people and through the temple into the world (Ezekiel 47:1–12), even so today it should flow from the church into the broader society. When the church fails to act in concert with God's prescribed agenda, then God often chooses to postpone His active involvement until His people are prepared to respond. Our failure to respond to this issue of racial unity has allowed what never should have been a problem in the first place to continue for hundreds of years.

What has clearly been lacking in American Christianity is our collective ability to clearly understand and function from a kingdom perspective. A kingdom perspective urges us to open our eyes, hearts, and minds in order to take what we learn about ourselves, and from each other, with regard to the strengths inherent within each of us, and merge these together to form a more productive union.

Far too often, we have tried to *achieve* oneness through marginalizing racial distinctions rather than *embracing* them. This is because Christianity has made reconciliation its own goal. However, the purpose of reconciliation encompasses more than merely being able to articulate that we are one.

Reconciliation is not an end in itself.

Reconciliation is a means toward the greater end of bringing glory to God through seeking to advance His kingdom in a lost world. Therefore, authentic racial unity manifests itself through mutual relationship and service, not in seminars.

The church of Jesus Christ has on a large scale, with some exceptions, missed our calling. I would like to suggest that the church, while building great ministries and great buildings, has missed the kingdom.

If Christians can ever merge strength with strength in order to create a more complete whole, there will be no stopping the impact we can have not only in our nation, but in our world. Conversely, the absence of a unifying purpose that is larger than ourselves, a kingdom agenda,[2] will continue to keep us from having a transforming influence. This is because we will remain focused on each other, or ourselves, as the end result rather than on how we can amalgamate our uniquenesses and gifts together in order to accomplish our goal.

WRAPPING THE CHRISTIAN FAITH IN THE AMERICAN FLAG

For far too long white Christians have wrapped the Christian faith in the American flag, often creating a civil religion that is foreign to the way God intended His church to function. Our nation's founding fathers are frequently elevated to the level of church fathers in the arguments for the United States having been founded as a Christian nation.

While we should celebrate and affirm the Judeo-Christian worldview that influenced the framework for the founding of our nation and the Constitution, we must also be careful to judge our nation's founders by their application of that same worldview. Our founding fathers' failure to apply the principles of freedom that they were espousing to the area of race is a prominent reason why many minority individuals today are less than enthusiastic to join in with those in our nation who want to exalt or restore America's history and heritage.

Further, what is often missing in our appeal to return to the heritage and faith of our founding fathers is an acknowledgment and reversal of a major theological contradiction that many held—that of proclaiming justice for all while denying it for many. While much in our national history reflects the call to a biblical worldview on the rights endowed to us by our Creator, we have often appealed to that heritage while simultaneously ignoring the moral inconsistencies that were prevalent in its application.

This has also led to a failure to be fully informed about a major aspect of American history in general, and church history in particular. It is common, for example, for Christian colleges to teach church history with limited or even no meaningful reference to the black church at all, thus keeping students from getting the whole truth about the history of our faith and of our nation. It is also common for our secular institutions all the way down to elementary schools to leave out critical pieces of history which reinforce strengths within the African-American culture, outside of Black History Month.

I am convinced that many of the social issues plaguing the black community today are due to the vast majority of blacks who have never heard the truth regarding our racial origins, development, and historical accomplishments. When people do not fully know who they are and where they come from, they become more vulnerable to allowing someone else to define these and like issues for them. Also, when members of other ethnic groups do not fully know the value of black culture and black church history, they are left with a limited definition steeped in stereotypical generalizations of who we are as people.

WRAPPING THE CHRISTIAN FLAG IN BLACK CULTURE

While white Christians have frequently wrapped the Christian faith in the American flag, black Christians have also merged tradition with faith by wrapping the Christian flag in black culture. At times, this has been done to such a degree that it has led to a failure in making the necessary distinctions that should reflect a kingdom-based approach to life. How else can you explain the overwhelming acceptance of musical and comedic artists who have some of the most lewd lyrics and degrading statements in their performances about the opposite sex while concurrently thanking their Lord and Savior Jesus Christ? What's worse is the amount of applause that comes from this overwhelmingly "Christian" audience, both live and at home, at this illegitimate union of faith and culture.

It is this absence of accountability and righteous judgment that keeps many in the black community from experiencing and fully realizing God's kingdom purpose for us in spite of the mammoth amount of God-given talent and creative genius with which our Creator has endowed us. The disconnect between what is professed on Sunday and what is lived out from Monday through Saturday limits our individual and collective progress.

While some of the challenges we face in the black community truly stem from the past and its personal and systemic aftermath, there are also many challenges that stem from our failure to properly take responsibility for and be held accountable to our actions, morality, families, the quality of services that we provide as well as the proper management of our human and financial resources. Wrong is to be judged and changed, not applauded and excused with no consequences.

I acknowledge that racism is real, and it is also systemic. But it is not an excuse for irresponsible behavior, family abandonment, or not taking advantage of what is available in creating steps for moving forward. Just like an offense on a sports team can't use the defense as an excuse not to try to score, a person cannot use racism as an excuse not to call a better play in their own life choices.

While not seeking to diminish the impact of racism upon a culture, I also want us to recognize that illegitimate or continual cries of racism are self-limiting and self-defeating. They simply foster a victim mentality that reinforces a pathology of dependency. Victimology can be defined as *nurturing an unfocused strain of resentment rooted in a defeatist identity through which all realities are filtered, rather than viewing challenges as opportunities to overcome*. It is virtually impossible to be a victor and a victim at the same time. In God's kingdom, victimology negates the foundational theological truths of sovereignty and victory in Christ (Romans 8:28, 37).

RIGHTEOUSNESS <u>AND</u> JUSTICE

It is my contention that at the core of the problem of racial disunity in America is the failure to understand and execute a kingdom-based theology on both righteousness and justice. Righteousness refers to personal responsibility in keeping with God's standard while justice refers to that same standard in our relationships with others. A balance between the two is

WHEN EITHER RIGHTEOUSNESS *OR* JUSTICE IS MISSED OR REDUCED IN SIGNIFICANCE, THEN THE INDIVIDUAL, FAMILY, CHURCH, AND SOCIETY WILL BE OUT OF BALANCE.

🐦 #WeCanDoBetter

absolutely critical since it is from God's kingdom throne that both righteousness and justice originate (Psalm 89:14).

White Christians, with all of their strengths, often focus on personal righteousness at the exclusion of biblical justice. However, there exists within that scope a limited definition of personal righteousness, since the practice of biblical justice is an essential part of living a life of personal righteousness. This limited definition is why a pastor can be fired for immorality, but not for allowing segregation or other forms of injustice either through acts of omission or commission.

On the other hand, while there is much within black culture that is to be celebrated, black Christianity sometimes emphasizes social justice at the expense of personal responsibility. What is worse is that when blacks take a viewpoint to address personal responsibility in the national media or platform, they are often dismissed or vilified by our own people for resisting an automatic appeal to racism as the dominant, or only, influencer and issue.

The balance between righteousness and justice is crucial in that God's commitment to bring His kingdom benefits to bear on one generation is tied to training the next generation in how to function effectively with it (Genesis 18:19). When either righteousness *or* justice is missed or reduced in significance, then the individual, family, church, and society will be out of balance.

THE CONTRADICTION OF LIBERTY

During my college summers, I lived and worked in Philadelphia. I regularly set up tent, church, or outdoor crusades in that city. Frequently, I was able to participate in more than the logistics of the event, but also had the opportunity to do what I am passionate about doing, which is to posit the truth of God through preaching.

I have always been drawn to the truth. Truth, at its core, is God's view of a matter. It is a powerful entity able to transform lives both in history and for eternity. While truth includes information and facts, it also includes original intent, making it the absolute, objective standard by which reality is measured. The presence of truth brings clarity and understanding. Its absence leads to confusion and the presence of cognitive dissonance—holding contradictory ideas simultaneously.

Located in this same city of Philadelphia where I once preached as a young man is a perfect example of such a contradiction rising out of the abyss of the absence of truth. Hung in the heart of the City of Brotherly Love is the Liberty Bell. Originally cast to commemorate the fifty-year anniversary of William Penn's Charter of Privileges, the quotation, "Proclaim Liberty throughout all the land unto *all* the inhabitants thereof," was especially suited to the circumstances surrounding the intent of the Charter and its anniversary. That quotation from Leviticus 25:10 came immediately after the command, "Consecrate the fiftieth year." It was followed by the statement, "It shall be a jubilee for you; each one of you is to return to his family property and each to his own clan" (NIV).

At this time in biblical history, according to this passage, all Jews who had been sold into slavery were set free (Leviticus 25:40–41). Not only was liberty a possibility in light of the Jubilee, but it was guaranteed. Liberty and the end of slavery were simultaneous realities, mutually dependent upon each other in relationship to the call for jubilee.

Yet at the time in America when the jubilee was inscribed on the side of the great bell, the liberty it announced had been aborted for many. Slavery continued with no foreseeable end, sanctioned not only by society but also by the church. Fifty years after William Penn's famous charter, our nation's bell proclaimed its own contradictory fifty-year jubilee, ringing out the bittersweet sounds of an emasculated freedom across the hilltops and prairies of our vast land.

THE BREAKING OF THE BELL

My friend Ray McMillan introduced me to the Liberty Bell as a perfect object lesson for America's racial divide. In addressing why "the bell won't ring," Ray describes the crack as a perfect illustration for how our distortion of the Christian history of our nation has helped to maintain the racial divide.

The Liberty Bell rang in celebration of momentous civic achievements or to summon people together for a special announcement. One of these achievements, according to tradition, was the first public reading of the Declaration of Independence on July 8, 1776. It is said that the sound of the Liberty Bell called out to citizens both far and near to join in this historic event. Rich and poor, well dressed and disheveled

WHAT MANY THOUGHT WOULD BRING RACIAL HEALING IN OUR LAND HAS ONLY BROUGHT TO LIGHT HOW DEEP THE RACIAL DIVIDE REALLY IS.

🐦 #WeCanDoBetter

came together as a community to hear the words,

> We hold these truths to be self-evident, that *all* men are created equal, that they are endowed by their Creator with certain unalienable Rights, that among these are Life, Liberty and the pursuit of Happiness.

The Declaration's truth rang deeply within those who heard it, echoing the resonant tones of the bell. For a moment in time, both the Declaration and the Bell proclaimed liberty together. Yet fissures, or cracks, in the bell, a reflection of fissures in the conscience of our land, raised the concern of those most closely working with it. Attempts were made to bore out the cracks before they developed into something more severe.

In 1846, in honor of George Washington's birthday, the bell rang faithfully for hours until ultimately succumbing to the pressure put upon the cracks. The *Philadelphia Public Ledger* reported that just after noon, the bell split widely on one side, rendering it unringable:

> The old Independence Bell rang its last clear note on Monday last in honor of the birthday of Washington and now hangs in the great city steeple irreparably cracked and dumb. . . . It gave out clear notes and loud, and appeared to be in excellent condition until noon, when it received a sort of compound fracture in a zigzag direction through one of its sides which put it completely out of tune and left it a mere wreck of what it was.[3]

In a city known for brotherly love, a compound fracture proclaimed otherwise. The jagged divide up the side of the symbol for equality and liberty could not be any more profound in its revelation of dualistic realities. There is a gap in the Liberty Bell, a missing point of connection preventing it from ringing clearly with the smooth tones of a complete union—of oneness.

Something is also missing in our nation today. The election of our first African-American president, and all that led up to it a number of years ago, reignited the discussion in our land on race relations and equality. What many thought would bring racial healing in our land has only brought to light how deep the racial divide really is. Whether it is reflected in racially activated acts of violence in the community or workplace or in political accusations between and within parties, racism has been re-introduced as an issue that simply hasn't been resolved.

Issues of race smolder beneath the news headlines of today in the areas of immigration reform, racial profiling, zoning issues, stop and frisk laws, and educational and economic disparity. The racial issue lies just below the surface, rising up above it as we've seen historically through events such as the Rodney King beating, the O.J. Simpson trial, and Trayvon Martin's death.

Yet beyond what is happening in our nation, and what concerns me personally even more, is that something is missing in the church.

Like the problem with the bell, a compound fracture has

zigzagged through the body of Christ, keeping us largely divided along racial and class lines. This division has existed for some time, and while attempts have been made to bore out the fissures through seminars, racial-reconciliation events, and well-intentioned efforts at creating experiences of unity, we have a long way to go toward strengthening the areas that have cracks or filling in the gaps that loom between us.

A BATTLE FOR FREEDOM

A battle is going on right now in our nation about the meaning of freedom. This battle concerns the role of the church. Often we are divided over politics. A battle between socialism and capitalism is seeking to divide our nation even further than it already is.

We, the church, have allowed these battles to divide people of faith even more deeply than before. We cannot afford this. Our nation cannot afford this. Our sons and daughters— whether black, white, or any other complexion—cannot afford this. We can no longer afford to sit idly by representing the body of Christ as a "mere wreck" of its divine design. The solutions to the issues we face today are found only by applying a biblical and divine standard as answers to the questions before us.

The church should be a model, at such a time as this, to reveal to the world what true oneness, equality, and freedom can produce. Hell advances on the church's doorsteps with fervent speed, and as long as we remain divided, it will continue to do so.

We can resist hell's advances and take back our communities for Christ if we are willing to come together by first filling in our own gaps—gaps in our understanding, our knowledge of our unique histories, and our relationships—while simultaneously repairing our own fissures that lead to even greater divides.

Our songs ring mournfully flat when the bells on our churches remain cracked. Even so, we continue to belt out our songs with tremendous passion at times, perhaps in hopes that by singing them loudly enough we can somehow cover the silence between us. We sing emotion-filled lyrics designed to draw us together by reminding us that "we all bleed red" until we are blue in the face. But the truth is that when the song is over, we go our separate ways.

We go our separate ways because we have discovered that it takes more than a hug or a friendly "hello" to bridge the gap. While some of us have, many of us have not taken the necessary effort to get to know each other on a level of an authentic exchange. Without a basis of shared knowledge, purposes, and mutual respect, we cannot come together for any meaningful impact.

With the racial divide still stretching wide for miles, we obviously haven't done enough. Much of what has gone on under the designation of racial reconciliation and oneness in Christianity is nothing more than tolerance. To be certain, we have come a long way from slavery, Jim Crow laws of segregation, and other overt expressions of racial hatred.

But tolerating each other does not mean we have reconciled.

The two are not the same, as demonstrated by the fact that we remain relationally separated most of the time, only coming together for a scheduled event as opposed to living out a desire for ongoing mutual edification and implementation of a shared vision.

The proof that we still have a long way to go in the church today is that a collective cross-cultural presence is not having a restoring effect in our society. We are more concerned about achieving the American dream than we are about letting the rule of God remake segregated churches and denominations. In so doing, we have limited the degree to which the healing balm of God's grace flows freely from us into our communities, and ultimately throughout our land. If what we call racial reconciliation is not transforming individuals, families, churches, and communities, then it is merely sociology with a little Jesus sprinkled on top.

Biblical racial reconciliation may be defined as *addressing the sin that caused the divide for the purpose of bonding together across racial lines based on a shared commitment to Jesus Christ with the goal of service to others.*

In a nation whose middle name is "Me" and where "time is money," being intentional about relationships is required even when connecting with others in our own culture. The very structure of our society impedes many of us in our pursuit of making authentic connections. This is even more so when it comes to developing relationships with others in a different culture than our own. But unity, as we will see through a careful study of Scripture, is worth the effort. This is because

IF THE TRUTH IS SUPPOSED TO SET US FREE AND YET WE ARE STILL NOT FREE FROM ENORMOUSLY DESTRUCTIVE RACIAL AND CLASS DIVISIONS IN THE CHURCH, THEN THE TRUTH IS MISSING.

🐦 #WeCanDoBetter

unity is the preeminent vehicle through which God displays not only His power and His presence, but also His glory.

If the truth is supposed to set us free and yet we are still not free from enormously destructive racial and class divisions in the church, then the truth is missing.

The result of this missing truth in our history and culture has kept segments of the black community looking to governmental systems for assistance rather than taking personal initiative. This lack of initiative often comes cradled in a victim mentality where racism is blamed for many more things than it should be.

This missing truth has also kept segments of the white community in bondage to a relational style based on stereotypical presumptions as well as a paternalistic expectation birthed in a spirit of entitlement. This prohibits many white Christians from adopting and benefiting from a learning posture underneath black Christians, as well as assisting in the ending of systemic racism and its effects.

The result is a stronghold on both groups, keeping pockets of society chained within a prescribed framework, creating pathologies that continue and are reinforced generationally.

LOST IN THE QUAGMIRE

A lack of healthy dialogue, which includes listening, on the ever-present and always-real issue of race relations in our nation—along with a lack of mutual service—has kept us lost and at odds with one another in this discussion of racial, cultural, and class disparity.

My own story reflects this difficulty. I go into greater detail on my personal story in my book *Oneness Embraced*, but include some of it briefly here. What is important to note is that while my story is my own, it is not mine alone. It is not unique to me. My story mirrors countless others still being written on the pages of black lives. Whether there exists generational, class, educational, denominational, or even theological differences between us, one unifying theme that binds the black story together is that we all wrestle with reconciling the social and spiritual contradictions prevalent in American Christianity.

Growing up in urban America in a Christian context during a time of racism, segregation, and an incomplete historical education served to remind me in many ways that I was a second-class citizen. It was frustrating, painful, and confusing. There were places that I couldn't go and people with whom I couldn't associate simply because of the color of my skin. In fact, I was even told that I could expect to only go so far in my life because that was the nature of my created being.

These experiences were powerfully negative and caused me to struggle with my sense of identity. In much the same way that the gaping crack in the Liberty Bell represented a contradiction within realities—that of freedom for *all* in the midst of racism and segregation for *some*—I struggled to connect the social reality presented to me as that of being less than someone else with the spiritual reality that Jesus loved me so much that He died for me. I wrestled in an attempt to come to grips with whether or not I was required to accept this second-class rendering that I was hearing in so many different directions about *who* I was and *why* I was.

What I witnessed in the church only reinforced this conundrum concerning truth. Some of my professors in college and in seminary would either attend or pastor a segregated church while at the same time teaching a theology on the oneness of the body of Christ. It forced me, and many others, to seek out an authentic understanding of biblical theology rooted and grounded in absolute truth. It forced me to dig deeply to discover what God had to say about the situation, rather than passively accept the contradiction.

Did God want me to give up my culture, background, and history in order to make it in a society that would not embrace me as I was? Or did He want me to see myself as He sees me—a child intentionally designed by His creative abilities whom He has positioned within two cultures?

Experiencing urban America at the height of the civil rights movement and the formation and implementation of black power and black theology has afforded me a perspective on race distinct to my own culture. However, studying theology for nine years in a white evangelical institution, as well as being the first African-American to graduate with a ThD from that same institution, has afforded me a keen view into the theological thinking of white Christians. Through both realms, I learned how to analyze and apply the theology I was being taught.

My perspective for the writing and teaching I do on race, then, and my perspective for all I do with regard to a kingdom agenda philosophy for ministry, flows out of this diverse locus. It is my attempt to tie reality to Scripture and demonstrate how the Bible reveals that the church and society should address matters of race and social justice.

In doing so, I speak not only to others in the church and society, but also to myself and those like me who have had to wrestle with reconciling the schisms between America's social and spiritual actualities.

As a committed Christian, I am tightly tethered to Scripture as my final authority on all matters to which it speaks. And it speaks on all matters. I am committed to the thesis that there are two answers to every question—God's answer and everyone else's. And when they contradict each other, everyone else is wrong.

As a black Christian, my vision was formed in the pragmatic reality of racial disparity that caused me to focus on questions about race, oneness, and justice in church history that many of my white counterparts did not have to address. This dualism forced me to read Scripture to shed light on these issues, leading me to the conclusions that are being put forward in the pages you are reading now. I had to look not only to the theology but also the practical application of that theology within the *Sitz im Leben*—or situation in life—for how that theology fleshes out.

These words are my attempt to put on paper this reference point, detailing how it applies to both blacks and whites with regard to racial unity in the body of Christ. Our unity will then serve as a template for bringing about a comprehensive solution to the results of racial disparity, and its resultant effects, in our communities.

Until we see ourselves, and each other, as God sees us, and respond with an intentional embracing of His mandate of oneness, we will forever ring flat in a world that longs to hear the liberating cadence of truth.

AS A WHITE CHRISTIAN—HOW CAN I DO BETTER?

Historically, white evangelicalism believed and taught many of the right things concerning unity in the body of Christ, but throughout time it did not consistently apply this belief system in either the church or the culture. While there have always been individuals in white culture who sought to apply the right practice of this belief—a remnant such as the Quakers, the abolitionists, and the white freedom marchers, among others—they did not always have a paradigm through which to express it, nor do they always have that today.

There has existed a dichotomy, making it difficult to apply the truth of racial unity, alongside biblical justice. As Dr. Warren Wiersbe, renowned white Bible teacher and father to many in the ministry, acknowledged, this roadblock often led to an ignoring of these and like issues in the white church.

He wrote,

> We are handicapped in the white church. If I preached
> Jesus' first sermon (Luke 4:14–30) and gave it the social
> emphasis that He gave, our church has no vehicle for doing
> anything about the problem. People would respond in one
> of two ways: 1) "This preacher is off-base, so let's get rid
> of him," or 2) "I've never seen it quite that way, but what
> do I do next?" For the most part, our white churches don't
> have the instruments, the organizational structure, to get
> involved in social action. Our usual solution is to put some
> inner-city organization into the budget or maybe to collect
> and distribute used clothing. . . . When it comes to racial
> issues, many white churches will participate in any number
> of symbolic activities, but they're hesitant when you ask
> them to get involved in sacrificial services in the trenches.[4]

Although difficulties and challenges exist, their presence
should never be the criteria for whether we give up or keep
trying. Views of theology formed through the lens of any culture will not only produce a distorted view, but also will result
in an inability to carry out the true teaching in Scripture.

This inability not only affects those who would be the re-
cipients of the ministry outreaches, but it also affects those doing the ministry because it limits God's involvement in what
is being done. Only when truth is the absolute standard by
which thoughts and actions are aligned will we experience the
full manifestation of God's glory, purposes, and plans in the

body of Christ. Maintaining an informational view of theology while neglecting a holistic view of God's kingdom aborts any real opportunity for application. Learning how to submit one's cultural traditions to the authority of God's Word will play a key part in dismantling the racial mythology that is a dominant theme in many people's worldview.

In addition, the white Christian community must seek to hold their own community accountable for justice—for equal treatment under the law. A cursory glance at many of the statistics indicate that there still exists a dual standard. Both the police officers and the media's response to two seven-year-old boys, one white and one black, who chose to illegally drive, reveals this standard in an ominous way. I've not gone into further depth on these instances for sake of space but for more information, visit the link in the notes section.[5]

Because of this limited and often distorted worldview, whites are sometimes hindered from seeing beyond skin to discover the qualitative benefits that would come their way through using and learning from the skills, intellect, and creativity of their black brothers and sisters.

In the same way that the realm of athletics was enhanced by the participation of blacks, the kingdom of God would be much more holistically advanced if there were a recognition and use of the gifts, talents, and unique qualities of black Christians. But in order for that to take place, there must be a willingness on the part of white Christians to not only give access to but also intentionally pursue, or respond to an invitation for, ongoing relationships and ministry partnerships with their brothers and sisters in Christ.

Yet, that said, some of you reading this book may not have the opportunity to reach across racial lines to form partnerships of reconciliation simply due to the demographics of your local town. I realize that. You may live in an area that is made up of a single cultural group. Yet there are still ways in which you can engage in very positive ways in this discussion.

I would encourage you to bring the National Church Adopt-A-School Initiative to your area. All communities—regardless of size—are experiencing corrosion and hopelessness, resulting in decadent behavior and negative community norms. You can play an active part through this initiative in bring hope and healing to your community.

For larger suburban churches that have the means, I encourage you to support urban churches that might reside in the same town, or a nearby town, that want to establish adopt-a-school programs. Over the years, we have received the gracious support of two prominent white churches in the North Dallas area: Prestonwood Baptist Church in Plano, Texas, and Gateway Church in Southlake, Texas. They have been a great blessing to us, but it is my prayer that we have blessed them as well in the relationship.

Keep in mind that many urban churches may not have access to the resources necessary to carry out the adopt-a-school plan at the level that they desire. Larger churches may be able to provide potential board members; access to funding sources (many corporate and foundation leaders attend large churches in suburban communities); leadership training; staff development; in-kind donations of furniture, equipment, and supplies; mission support; volunteers; a system of fiscal controls; facility acquisition and more.

Although there might be a physical distance between you and your partnership with an urban church, you still have the opportunity to make a real and lasting impact in the lives of those in need.

For those churches that may not want to adopt this specific ministry model, I want to encourage you to implement some form of good works in your community that benefits the broader society and gives an opportunity to share the gospel. Intentionally serving across racial lines will give a greater opportunity to experience real unity while accomplishing good in the lives of others.

And for those individuals who want to take steps toward practicing biblical oneness in the body of Christ but are unable to implement such a comprehensive plan, consider volunteering your time at a school or church across racial lines, if possible, to provide some of the services outlined in our training materials.

Whatever you choose to do, it will make a difference in the lives of others.

AS A BLACK CHRISTIAN—HOW CAN I DO BETTER?

The mentality of reconciliation is as important for blacks as it is for whites. If black Christians wish to be viewed as equals then we must function as equals. That means we must view ourselves as having something to offer, not just there to receive. It means we come to the table of reconciliation not for others to do for us, but for them to join with us. It means we come to the table not as victims, but as equals. It also means that there cannot be double standards in race relations.

In a recent survey, it was found that more Americans view blacks as racist than either whites or Hispanics. Thirty-seven percent of the cross-racial polled group said that blacks are racist, and 31 percent of the black polled group said the same thing.[6] If we are going to set about to create any meaningful improvement in our cultures and communities, we are going to need to see each other, across racial boundaries, as brothers and sisters in Christ.

In addition, we need to hold each other accountable, as well as those who influence us such as actors, entertainers, musicians, and leaders to a high standard of respect toward one another and decency in dress, language, and manners. When we don't, we are only hurting ourselves.

After all, nowhere is the demise of the family more obvious than in urban America in general and the black community in particular. The crisis in the culture at large has become a catastrophe among black people.

At one time, our community provided one of the best il-lustrations of biblical family life that our world has ever seen. Taking their cue from the Old Testament, black neighbor-hoods operated like extended families. Almost everyone we knew was like an aunt, uncle, or cousin. The elderly were treated with utmost respect, and everyone held everyone else accountable for proper behavior.

Most amazingly, all this took place in some terribly inhumane environments. Yet in spite of slavery, Jim Crow, segregation, and discrimination, the black family was held together by an unshakable faith in God and a tenacious spirit rooted in hope. The church was the center of community life, bolstering the family. And the role models children needed lived next door or at worst a block away.

But times have changed. Today, the number one cause of death for black young men is homicide, more than car accidents, suicides, and diseases combined.[7] Over 70 percent of all black children are born to unwed mothers, and nearly 40 percent of all black children are being raised in poverty.[8] We now have a generation of women with not enough men to marry.

In days gone by, if the parents couldn't or wouldn't take care of their children, the grandparents would take them in. The children would thus receive the love and wisdom of their elderly grandparents. Today, however, Grandma is often between thirty-five and forty years old and single herself, struggling to survive and without the time or experience to provide the wisdom her grandchildren need. That reality has left us with a generation that in many ways must raise itself.

The price to our communities can be measured in loss of life, hope, property, and family stability. We are contributing to our own demise. The entertainment industry is assisting in our implosion by raising up the wrong heroes in rap music and movies—that which gets the limelight is leading our younger generations down the path of destruction.

Our challenge is to stop giving excuses for why we can't

change things and start determining how we will change things. We don't have a resource problem. Nor are we deficient in the necessary intellect or skills. The solutions to our problems are sitting in our pews, and within ourselves.

If the black community is to be rebuilt, we must start with a change of attitude. Rather than spending so much time talking about how bad things are, we must begin to look for and operate out of our own strengths. That means we must stop depending on government to do for us what we are responsible to do for ourselves.

Racism is real and evil. It must be resisted and ultimately defeated. But racism has absolutely nothing to do with some of the things that it gets blamed for. Racism is not responsible for producing babies out of wedlock; illegitimate sex is. Nor is racism responsible for aborting those babies once they've been conceived. Racism isn't responsible for black-on-black crime; it doesn't pull the trigger. Racism doesn't keep our kids in front of the Internet, television, or computer games instead of in a textbook. Neither does racism make a man leave his family.

Admittedly, racism may create a climate where some of those evils flourish more easily, but we must never succumb to its influence. While racism must be addressed and fought, it cannot be allowed to keep us from doing what needs to be done for ourselves.

We should determine what our families would look like if racism didn't exist, and then go about building such families.

My parents didn't have access to a lot of family seminars and the newest Christian literature while my siblings and I were growing up; in those years, blacks were rarely included in major Christian outreaches at all. But they did have a Bible and a passionate love for Jesus Christ, each other, and their children—and somehow that was enough. Economic, racial, and class limitations need not be the last word in how children turn out.

The objective truth from Scripture must place limits on our cultural experiences. As blacks continue to seek cultural freedom, we must examine every strategy offered to promote social justice and policy under the magnifying glass of Scripture. Every bit of advice given by our leaders and all definitions proposing to tell us what it means to be black must be commensurate with divine revelation. If what we are given as cultural is not biblically acceptable, it cannot be accepted as authoritative.

The mission of every black church (as well as any ethnicity), then, should be to mobilize its members to use their skills for ministry to their community. The problem is that many church members don't understand it's their job to do the work of ministering. Doctors are supposed to doctor for the kingdom. Teachers are teachers for the kingdom. Administrators are to administrate for the kingdom. Like no other group in America, we have both the ability and the historical experience to demonstrate to the culture at large how to save a generation.

We are too great a people with too great a God and too rich a heritage to have the kind of family and community disintegration we're now experiencing. It will take every ounce of our energy to reclaim our families and communities. But if not now, when? And if not us, who?

APPENDIX 2:
THE URBAN ALTERNATIVE

D r. Tony Evans and The Urban Alternative (TUA) **equips, empowers,** and **unites** Christians to **impact** *individuals, families, churches,* and *communities* to restore hope and transform lives.

We believe the core cause of the problems we face in our personal lives, homes, churches, and societies is a spiritual one; therefore, the only way to address them is spiritually. We've tried a political, a social, an economic, and even a religious agenda. It's time for a Kingdom Agenda—God's visible and comprehensive rule over every area of life—because when we function as we were designed, there is a divine power that changes everything. It renews and restores as the life of Christ is made manifest within our own. As we align ourselves under Him, there is an alignment that happens from deep within— where He brings about full restoration. It is an atmosphere that revives and makes whole.

As it impacts us, it impacts others—transforming every

sphere of life in which we live. When each biblical sphere of life functions in accordance with God's Word, the outcomes are evangelism, discipleship, and community impact. As we learn how to govern ourselves under God, we then transform the institutions of family, church, and society from a biblically based kingdom perspective where, through Him, we are touching heaven and changing earth.

To achieve our goal we use a variety of strategies, methods, and resources for reaching and equipping as many people as possible.

BROADCAST MEDIA

Hundreds of thousands of individuals experience *The Alternative with Dr. Tony Evans* through the daily radio broadcast playing on nearly **1,000 radio outlets** and in over **130 countries**. The broadcast can also be seen on several television networks, and is viewable online at TonyEvans.org.

LEADERSHIP TRAINING

The Kingdom Agenda Pastors (KAP) provides a *viable network* for *like-minded pastors* who embrace the Kingdom Agenda philosophy. Pastors have the opportunity to go deeper with Dr. Tony Evans as they are given greater biblical knowledge, practical applications, and resources to impact individuals, families, churches, and communities. KAP welcomes *senior and associate pastors* of all churches.

The Kingdom Agenda Pastors' Summit progressively develops

church leaders to meet the demands of the 21st century while maintaining the Gospel message and the strategic position of the church. The Summit introduces *intensive seminars, workshops,* and *resources,* addressing issues affecting the community, family, leadership, organizational health, and more.

Pastors' Wives Ministry, founded by Dr. Lois Evans, provides *counsel, encouragement,* and *spiritual resources* for pastors' wives as they serve with their husbands in the ministry. A primary focus of the ministry is the KAP Summit that offers senior pastors' wives a safe place to *reflect, renew,* and *relax* along with training in personal development, spiritual growth, and care for their emotional and physical well-being.

COMMUNITY IMPACT

National Church Adopt-A-School Initiative (NCAASI) prepares churches across the country to impact communities by using *public schools as the primary vehicle for effecting positive social change* in urban youth and families. Leaders of churches, school districts, faith-based organizations, and other nonprofit organizations are equipped with the knowledge and tools to *forge partnerships* and build *strong social service delivery systems.* This training is based on the comprehensive church-based community impact strategy conducted by Oak Cliff Bible Fellowship. It addresses such areas as economic development, education, housing, health revitalization, family renewal, and racial reconciliation. We also assist churches in tailoring the model to meet the specific needs of their communities while simultaneously addressing the spiritual and moral frame of reference.

RESOURCE DEVELOPMENT

We are fostering lifelong learning partnerships with the people we serve by providing a variety of published materials. We offer booklets, Bible studies, books, CDs, and DVDs to strengthen people in their walk with God and ministry to others.

* * *

For more information,
a catalog of Dr. Tony Evans' ministry resources,
and a complimentary copy of
Dr. Evans' devotional newsletter,
call (800) 800-3222
or write TUA at P.O. Box 4000, Dallas TX 75208,
or log on to
www.TonyEvans.org

NOTES

1. Conducted by John Roman, a senior fellow at the Urban Institute's Justice Policy Center http://www.pbs.org/wgbh/pages/frontline/criminal-justice/is-there-racial-bias-in-stand-your-ground-laws/.

2. Tony Evans, *The Kingdom Agenda*, (Chicago, IL: Moody Publishers, 2013).

3. "The Old Independence Bell," *The Philadelphia Public Ledger*, February 26, 1846. www.ushistory.org/libertybell/

4. E. K. Bailey and Warren W. Wiersbe, *Preaching in Black and White: What We Can Learn from Each Other* (Grand Rapids, Mich.: Zondervan, 2003), 105.

5. Lisa Wade, "Two 7-Year-Old Boys, Two Dramatically Different News Stories", *Huffington Post,* August 8, 2013, http://www.huffingtonpost.com/2013/07/22/media-kids-racial-stereotypes_n_3624740.html.

6. Scott Rasmussen, "More Americans View Blacks as Racist than Whites, Hispanics", *Rasmussen Reports,* July 3, 2013, http://www.rasmussenreports.com/public_content/lifestyle/general_lifestyle/july_2013/more_americans_view_blacks_as_racist_than_whites_hispanics.

7. Scott Travis, "Homicide Leading Cause of Death of Young Black Men, Says FAU Researcher", *Huffington Post*, April 10, 2013, http://www.huffingtonpost.com/2013/04/10/leading-cause-of-death-young-black-men-homicide_n_3049209.html.

8. Jason M. Breslow, "By the Numbers: Childhood Poverty in the U.S.", *Frontline*, November 20, 2012, http://www.pbs.org/wgbh/pages/frontline/social-issues/poor-kids/by-the-numbers-childhood-poverty-in-the-u-s/.

ONENESS EMBRACED

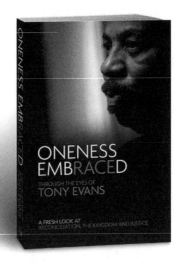

Martin Luther King Jr. once pointed out that Sunday morning at 11am is the most segregated hour in America. In this legacy work by Dr. Tony Evans, Oneness Embraced offers a kingdom perspective which teaches the need for Christians to embrace our diversity in Christ, and as we do so, we form a more perfect union. This is what God calls Oneness.

This masterpiece is a rare and candid glimpse into the unique backdrop that positioned Dr. Evans as a theologian between two diverse worlds—that of black culture and white mainline evangelicalism. Topics of unity, cultural and church history, the kingdom, social justice, and outreach are covered in this trusted work, giving us a personal look into the nature, purpose, and power of Oneness.

ISBN: 978-0-8024-1790-9   Hardback   Moody Publishers

Also available as an ebook

MOODY
PUBLISHERS

www.MoodyPublishers.com

#WeCanDoBetter

His intent was that now, through the church, the manifold wisdom of God should be made known..." Ephesians 3:10

Churches have been uniquely called to impact our society for good. In this timely and companion resource, Dr. Tony Evans offers "the plan" we have all been looking for to not only bring about racial unity in our country but to also restore our communities. He unveils a local model for the church that will impact your community and effect change in the lives of many. This step-by-step plan is sure to transform communities, and our nation.

ISBN: 978-0-8024-1181-5   Paperback   Moody Publishers

Also available as an ebook

MOODY
PUBLISHERS

www.MoodyPublishers.com